SAN FRANCISCO
A PICTURE MEMORY

Text
Bill Harris

Captions
Louise Houghton

Design
Teddy Hartshorn

Photography
Colour Library Books Ltd
FPG International
The Telegraph Colour Library
International Stock Photo

Commissioning Editor
Andrew Preston

Editorial
Gill Waugh

Production
Ruth Arthur
David Proffit
Sally Connolly

Director of Production
Gerald Hughes

Director of Publishing
David Gibbon

CLB 2509
© 1990 Colour Library Books Ltd, Godalming, Surrey, England.
All rights reserved.
Colour separations by Scantrans Pte Ltd.
This 1991 edition published by Crescent Books,
distributed by Outlet Book Company, Inc, a Random House Company,
225 Park Avenue South, New York, New York 10003.
Printed and bound in Hong Kong.
ISBN 0 517 01751 2
8 7 6 5 4 3 2

SAN FRANCISCO

A PICTURE MEMORY

CRESCENT BOOKS
NEW YORK

On June 27, 1776, as Thomas Jefferson was putting the finishing touches to the Declaration of Independence at Philadelphia, American history was also being made the width of a continent away. An expedition of Spanish Conquistadores, including a sergeant, two corporals, ten soldiers and two priests, was being led by Lieutenant José Morago to the edge of San Francisco Bay. They were looking to find a spot to build a settlement.

They weren't the first Europeans to see the bay. That accomplishment is credited to Captain Gaspar de Portolá, who had led an expedition there seven years earlier. But Gaspar was looking for a smaller harbor further up the coast and considered this one an obstacle in his path. He didn't bother trying to go around it, but turned around and went back to San Diego. It's hard to imagine why he wasn't excited about finding one of the world's greatest natural harbors, but easy to understand why he didn't want to go around it. It extends inland for more than thirteen miles and is over twenty-five miles wide. Portolá was a soldier, not a sailor.

And why, you might ask, hadn't the Spanish navy found this place on its own? After all, its ships had been sailing up and down the coast of California for more than 200 years by 1776. Not only that, but the great English explorer Sir Francis Drake had been in the territory, too. Back in 1579, he had discovered the little bay that Portolá was searching for and claimed it for his Queen. How could they all have missed a 400-square-mile body of water protected by hills as much as 900 feet high?

The hills are part of the answer. They do a good job of hiding what's behind them. And the relatively narrow channel that connects the bay to the sea is usually hidden under a fog bank. Today the hills and the fog are among the things that make San Francisco so charming. But back in the 16th century they prompted Spanish captains to echo the immortal words of Christopher Columbus and order their men to "Sail on!"

God alone knows how much longer those hills would have kept their secret if the Spanish authorities in Mexico City hadn't decided that the time had finally come to send their missionaries north. The Franciscans established themselves at San Diego in 1769 and began a slow march up the coast. San Francisco Bay was an obvious place to build one of their fortified missions, and on October 4, 1776, the Feast of St. Francis, they dedicated the place to their patron.

But the Saint wasn't smiling on them. Within a year almost all of the original settlers had pushed on further north, where their farms would be more productive. The little Mission of San Francisco was written off as a failure. The Presidio, the fort that protected it, was reduced to a handful of soldiers. During the War of 1812, British and American ships put in to the harbor, and there were occasional visits from Russian ships engaged in the fur-trade further north. But to all intents and purposes, San Francisco was quite literally a backwater during its first half-century as part of the "Known World."

When Mexico won its independence from Spain in 1821, it abandoned the outpost, which was in ruins by the time the Englishman Captain William Richardson built a combination house and trading post there fourteen years later. It may have been a ramshackle affair made of rough boards, but it was the beginning of a city.

Word had spread that California was a veritable Garden of Eden by then, and it wasn't long before Captain Richardson had plenty of neighbors. But growth was still slow. The Mexican authorities did all they could to keep foreigners out, but they were quickly outnumbered by radical Yankees. These same radicals took advantage of the 1846 war between Mexico and the United States to declare California a republic. The American flag was raised over the settlement they called Yerba Buena and the crew of an American fighting ship went ashore to start building a fort in case the Mexicans took it into their heads to come back.

The ship's officers also drafted a set of laws for the town and ordered that its name be changed back to San Francisco. But even though they had chosen a Spanish-sounding name, there was no mistaking the fact that this was going to be an American city. All that was needed now was something to lure Americans to settle there. The catalyst, of course, turned out to be gold. But during the first few months following its discovery further north in 1848 the whole population of San Francisco seemed determined to get out of town. Sailors deserted their ships, shopkeepers shuttered their stores, laborers decided their labors would be more profitable elsewhere. Things got so bad that the town's first newspaper, the *Californian*, was forced to suspend publication. Its editor wrote, "... the field is left half-planted, the house half-built and everything neglected but the manufacture of shovels and pick-axes and the means of transportation to the spot ... where the average for all concerned is twenty dollars per diem."

But there were some keys to success in those words.

The town may have been deserted, but the harbor was filled with cargo-laden ships and before long the gold was finding its way back to San Francisco. In less than six months nearly a million-dollars-worth of gold dust settled on the tiny city by the bay. The first equation to register among local businessmen was that the gold they were accumulating would soon be devalued by the law of supply and demand. So, they decided the best way to get the most out of it was to spend it quickly. When winter arrived in 1848, the miners flocked back to the relative comfort of San Francisco. They willingly paid twenty dollars a night and more for a bed to sleep in, usually the same bed that was occupied by someone else during the day. There wasn't much for any of them to do, but before long gambling rooms were established to separate them from their gold dust just that little bit faster. And the town that had begun as a Christian mission began to take on a veneer of wickedness.

Meanwhile, back East word was getting around that there was gold for the taking in this new El Dorado. Thousands joined wagon trains headed across the prairies, but thousands more decided that the best way to get to California was by boat. For them, of course, the only gateway to the gold-fields was San Francisco.

The West is filled with towns that boomed during gold and silver strikes, but died as quickly as they had grown. San Francisco had a very different destiny. In the beginning it was a collection of makeshift tents and rough wooden shacks, but these were destroyed in periodic fires and inevitably replaced by finer structures. The miners were removed to the Sierra Nevada, coming back to the city only to escape the winter or to stash their gold dust. The people who preferred to stay in the city were dedicated to outfitting and entertaining them, and it was good business sense to provide a cosmopolitan setting. By 1851, San Francisco was one of the most attractive cities on the continent, and a year or two later it was clearly entitled to become the western destination of the transcontinental railroad. In the meantime it was served by regularly scheduled stagecoaches from St. Louis, and by 1861 it had been connected to the rest of the country by telegraph lines. When the railroad finally did arrive eight years later, it brought a guarantee that San Francisco would never, ever become a ghost town.

By 1875, less than a hundred years after the Spanish Mission was established, the city's population had grown to a quarter-million. It had also become one of America's most popular tourist attractions. There was plenty to lure them, from a bawdy atmosphere to an exotic Chinese quarter, not to mention the opportunity to get rich quick speculating in mining stocks. There were more men selling stocks on streetcorners than there were newsboys peddling papers. Some tourists made more than the cost of their trip, though most just lost their shirts. But they didn't go hungry. Even in those early days San Francisco was famous for its restaurants. Some of them were elegant, charging as much as twenty dollars for a meal, but in most the average cost was down around twenty-five cents. And then there was that wonderful San Franciscan invention, the free lunch.

A guidebook writer noted in 1875 that "Nowhere else can a worthless fellow, too lazy to work, too cowardly to steal, get on so well. The climate befriends him, for he can sleep out of doors four-fifths of the year, and the free-lunch opens to him boundless vistas of carnal delights. ... There are two classes of place where these midday repasts are furnished – 'two bit' places and 'one bit' places. In the first he gets a drink and a meal; in the second he gets a drink and a meal of inferior quality. He pays (twenty-five to fifteen cents) for the drink and gets the meal for nothing. This consists, in the better class of establishments, of soup, boiled salmon, roast beef of the best quality, bread and butter, potatoes, tomatoes, crackers and cheese."

And these establishments weren't at all lacking in what food writers today call "ambience." The guidebook noted that "Many of the places are fitted up in a style of almost Oriental grandeur. A stranger entering one of them casually might labor under the delusion that he had found his way, by mistake, to the salon of a San Francisco millionaire. He would find mirrors reaching from floor to ceiling; carpets of the finest texture and the most exquisite patterns; luxurious lounges and arm chairs, massive tables covered with papers and periodicals; the walls embellished with expensive paintings." At that time, there were more than 300 such establishments in the city.

The designation "two bits" entered the American language in San Francisco. Nobody trusted paper money in the 1870s, and all they'd accept in San Francisco was gold or silver coins. But the coins didn't come in one-cent denominations, even though nearly all prices were established in terms of "bits," the value of which was twelve and a half cents. Two bits added up to a quarter of a dollar, but it was a rare merchant who could make change for anything smaller. The result was that a five-cent newspaper usually wound up costing a quarter, unless the buyer had had the foresight to be carrying the right change. But, of course, in the absence on one-cent coins, there was no such thing as the right change. If a customer offered a dime and a nickel in payment of something priced at one bit, he was out two and a half cents. If he offered just a dime, the merchant would reach for his gun. San Franciscans took the whole thing in their stride. Most of them felt it was beneath their dignity to carry anything but twenty-dollar goldpieces anyway.

Not everyone in San Francisco was rich, but those who weren't knew in their hearts that it was only a matter of time before they would be. And they were proud of the fact that their city had more millionaires per capita than any other in the United States. Then in the late 1870s, a new type appeared. A handful of men were beginning to count their fortunes in multiples of a million dollars. And they didn't accumulate a bit of it panning for gold.

From the time Europeans first discovered North America, men dreamed of using it as a route to the Orient. The development of San Francisco's harbor provided a kind of answer to the dream, and it quickly became America's most important port of entry for Chinese trade. But once the goods arrived, there was no way of getting them to where the markets were. The problem was solved by the transcontinental railroad, the prime mover of which at the San Francisco end was Collis P. Huntington. His cronies, Mark Hopkins, Leland Stanford and Charles Crocker had all been businessmen in the Sacramento area and had invested along with Huntington in a proposed railroad link with San Francisco. It would cut their cost of doing business after all. When the Federal Government agreed to put its money into a cross-country railroad, they didn't need much encouragement to broaden their horizons.

By then they had acquired every mile of track in the San Francisco-Oakland area, and controlled all of the intra-coastal water traffic and a sizeable part of trans-Pacific shipping. They were never the best of friends, but they shared the same lust for power and money; together they were unstoppable. It was only natural that they should all live in the same neighborhood and that their mansions should compete as statements of their respective owner's station in life. The neighborhood they developed was on Nob Hill. Their houses were without a doubt the most elegant, some said pretentious,

in the entire country, possibly the world.

Huntington chose the style of a French chateau for his house. Crocker on the other hand preferred to live in what resembled an Alpine hunting lodge, complete with seventy-five-foot-high tower from which to keep an eye on his transportation empire. Mark Hopkins turned to the Doge's Palace in Venice for his inspiration, but had the exterior resemble a medieval castle. Leland Stanford chose the current style of brooding Victorianism, though he added such trappings as plants mounted on elevators which would materialize or disappear at the press of a button.

In choosing shipping over mining, the barons of San Francisco had obviously done the right thing. By the time the gold gave out, the city was the third busiest seaport in the world. The boom town had faded away, and the city was on its way to becoming not only the commercial center, but the cultural capital of the Pacific Coast. Then, on April 18, 1906, disaster struck in the form of an earthquake and a fire that raged uncontrolled for seventy-two hours. Among the buildings destroyed was Mark Hopkins's medieval palace, which he had built of wood, but painted to look like stone. A New York newspaper reported, "The old San Francisco is dead. The gayest, lightest-hearted and most pleasure-loving city of the western continent, and in many ways the most interesting and romantic, is a horde of refugees living among ruins. It may rebuild; it probably will. But those who have known that peculiar city by the Golden Gate and have caught its flavor of the Arabian Nights, feel it can never be the same. It is as though a pretty, frivolous woman has passed through a great tragedy. She survives, but she is sobered and different." But like Mark Twain, who once responded to a premature obituary by saying, "Reports of my death are greatly exaggerated," San Francisco wasn't ready to be written off. The face of the frivolous woman may have been altered, but her heart was as strong as ever.

In the first months after the disaster, San Francisco resembled the city it had been at the beginning, with the 250,000 who had been left homeless living in tents or shacks. But before a year had passed, it was a boom town again. Within two more years more than 20,500 new buildings had been built, most of them bigger, better and handsomer than the ones they replaced. Many were technologically up-to-the-minute, having steel frame construction, a new idea back then. In fact, more than half the steel-frame buildings in the entire country at that time had San Franciscan addresses. And by the time the Panama Canal began making the trip from the Atlantic Ocean easier in 1915, San Francisco was once again one of the most important cities in the United States. It had not only recaptured the flavor of the Arabian Nights, but had taken a bow in the direction of classical elegance in its architecture. The new Civic Center and the buildings for the Panama-Pacific International Exposition marked the end of the rebuilding and the beginning of San Francisco's new lease of life.

The building didn't stop there, of course. It wasn't until 1936 that the Golden Gate and the Oakland Bay bridges were added to the scene. And the Opera House that provided the setting for the drafting of the United Nations charter in 1946 only dates back to 1932. In the late 1960s, when San Francisco was the world capital of hippiedom, the Establishment asserted itself through the construction of a new downtown business center. This culminated in the pyramid-shaped headquarters of the Transamerica Corporation, on the block-square site of the only buildings to survive the 1906 disaster. The building boom also included the less dramatic but taller

headquarters of the Bank of America, the world's richest bank. The history of this institution is almost as unusual as that of the city itself. It was begun in 1902 by Amadeo Peter Giannini, the son of an Italian immigrant who came to San Francisco as a fruit and vegetable peddler. His bank wasn't considered serious competition by any of the big operators. In fact, he couldn't even afford a steel vault to protect his depositors' money. This turned out to be a blessing in disguise. During the fire that followed the great earthquake, while other bankers trusted their fireproof vaults to save their assets, Giannini was forced to rescue his. Before the fires had had time to burn out he was the only banker in town with any cash to lend for reconstruction.

The story of San Francisco is filled with tales of men like Giannini. It has always attracted people with a venturesome spirit, people who would never dream of putting the words "down" and "out" together. For most, this is the place where dreams come true. Even casual visitors get a sense of it. Which is one very important reason why it's every American's favorite city.

Facing page: the Transamerica Pyramid.

San Francisco is an exciting place, and a must to visit for those not lucky enough to live there. The varied and ever-changing skyline of this relatively small city is a constant wonder, and its forty-five square miles contain a melting pot of cultures, designs and local histories. San Francisco's bridges are grand and world-renowned, its streets notoriously hilly, its sky-scrapers perilously high-reaching. Overleaf: the Golden Gate Bridge.

San Francisco (these pages) is built on a peninsula, and so, despite its dynamism, the city has never quite lost that certain quality of isolation that characterized its early years as a settlement. Today, however, skyscrapers rise in place of the shanty towns of hopeful gold prospectors, and the city's population is given in millions, not hundreds. Well-traveled journalist and author Bayard Taylor (1825-78) once wrote of the booming city: "There has never been anything to parallel San Francisco, nor will there ever be. Like the magic seed of the Indian juggler that sprouted, blossomed and bore fruit before the very eyes of the onlooker, so San Francisco seems in one day to have accomplished the growth of half a century." One of the most remarkable and distinctive landmarks of the city is the Golden Gate Bridge (overleaf). Its single 4,200-foot span is a credit both to the engineering profession and to the pioneering spirit of the San Franciscans, who had been told it could not be built.

People come to relax down by the Bay (these pages), and when the sun is out, there are few more pleasant places in all the world. Facing page: the Balclutha, a metal-hulled square-rigger that is now a museum moored at Pier 43. Ghirardelli Square (below and below right), once a woolen mill and then a chocolate factory, now houses a multitude of galleries, theaters and restaurants. Right, above right and overleaf: Fisherman's Wharf, one of the city's main attractions. Above: Pier 39.

San Franciscans aren't deprived of parkland; even in the middle of the city there's greenery to be found in Union Square (below). Union Square lies at the center of the city's excellent shopping area, an area comparable to those of London and Paris for quality and variety. Left: a view of the city from Mission Dolores Park. Mission Dolores, established in 1776 as a place of worship and education for the Indians and now a museum, is the oldest intact building in San Francisco. Another of the city's grassy oases is the Golden Gate Park, which includes the famous Japanese Tea Gardens, the California Academy of Sciences and the delightful Conservatory (facing page).

San Francisco at night (these pages) is a spectacle almost without equal. The view from Twin Peaks (overleaf) extends right down Market Street to the Bay and over the water to the Berkeley and Oakland hills. The graceful swathes of the Bay Bridge's suspension section (above right) are brightly lit. The remainder of the bridge, from Yerba Buena Island to Oakland, is cantilevered. Facing page: the Transamerica Pyramid.

San Francisco's many unique features are what make it special. The hills account for many of its most unusual features, such as Lombard Street (above, facing page and overleaf), the "crookedest street in the world". The cable cars add charm and make traveling easier on Powell (below) and Hyde (left) streets. Alcatraz Island, site of the infamous federal penitentiary, now a museum, may be seen from Hyde Street. Above left: Coit Tower looking out over the city and (below left) downtown seen from Clay Street.

Relaxation is a San Franciscan specialty, and it seems that wherever you go there are tempting cafés (below) offering cool drinks, an ice cream and a place to rest from all that wearing sight seeing. The Cannery (facing page), situated between Fisherman's Wharf (right) and Ghirardelli Square, is a fine old red-brick assemblage of shops, galleries, restaurants and open spaces shaded by picturesque olive trees. Like Ghirardelli Square, the Cannery is a product of the thoughtful restoration and adaptation of historic buildings to meet the changing needs of the city. Fisherman's Wharf itself is a hive of activity, and has been for over a century. The evocative aromas of fresh-caught fish, sourdough bread and the sea make the wharf a very special place. There are few experiences to match being down by the shore in San Francisco at night; an abundance of bars, restaurants and clubs ensure no-one is short of entertainment. Overleaf: the Golden Gate Bridge.

Looking at San Francisco from the air, it is easy to spot the landmarks that define the city. Above: Lombard Street wriggles its way from Hyde to Leavenworth. The Transamerica Pyramid and numerous other skyscrapers (below and above right) distinguish the horizon downtown; the Golden Gate (facing page bottom) and Bay (facing page top) bridges put the seal on it – this is unmistakeably San Francisco. Overleaf: the city seen from Interstate 80.

San Francisco's Chinatown (these pages and overleaf), roughly bordered by Stockton Street to the west, Columbus Avenue to the north, Kearny Street to the east and California Street (below) to the south, is home to the largest Chinese population outside Asia. Left and below left: Grant Avenue, where there are many superb restaurants.

Other cities in America may boast of their Victorian architectural heritage, but none of them come close to San Francisco. Many of the city's Victorian structures are preserved in the interests of local history. These pages and overleaf: witch's hat turrets and gabled windows, wooden porticos and decorative facades, all characteristics of the style. Columbus Avenue crosses the downtown grid on a diagonal, creating some unusual blocks – such as that (above) at the intersection with Pacific Avenue.

Dunsmuir House (facing page top and above), nestling in a valley of the Oakland Hills, was built in 1899 by Alexander Dunsmuir in the Classical Revival style. Facing page bottom and right: Whittier House on Jackson Street, the exquisitely furnished Richardson Romanesque headquarters of the California Historical Society. Below: the Eastlake-Queen Anne-style Haas Lilienthal House on Franklin Street. Above right: 1876 Lyford House on Richardson Bay, and (below right) Lathrop House, Redwood City.

San Francisco celebrated the opening of the
Panama Canal with the 1915 Panama-Pacific
Exposition, the only remnant of which, the
Palace of Fine Arts (these pages) stands at the
western edge of the Presidio. The remarkable
Neoclassical rotunda by Bernard Maybeck fell
into disrepair itself until, in 1958, it was
restored at the cost of two million dollars by
businessman Walter Johnson. Maybeck
designed the building to resemble "an old
Roman ruin away from civilisation." While it is
anything but away from civilisation, located as
it is just a short walk from the marina, the
Palace of Fine Arts nevertheless manages to
achieve that feeling of remoteness the architect
desired. Today it houses a science museum
called the Exploratorium.

Not far from San Francisco, in Muir Woods National Monument (below left), Marin County, giant redwoods (Sequoia sempervirens) may be found. A huge Buddha (above) seems quite at home in the Japanese Tea Gardens (remaining pictures), while pigeons appear to appreciate the tranquility of a pagoda (facing page).

When the old City Hall was destroyed in the 1906 earthquake, its destruction was seen as symbolizing the banishment of civic corruption and the beginning of a better county government – city and county are synonymous in San Francisco. The new building (facing page) is aptly Renaissance in style. Right: the Conservatory, the oldest building in Golden Gate Park, and (below) the Mormon Temple in Oakland.

Stanford University (these pages) in Berkeley was founded in 1885 by Senator and Mrs Leland Stanford as a memorial to their son. The University is a magnificent and revered seat of learning with an impressive history. Above left: the entrance to the campus, (left) the courtyard of the Old Union, and (below left) the northeast corner of the Inner Quadrangle (below). The grounds feature fruitless date palms (above) and sculptures (facing page) by the Hoover Tower. Overleaf: Memorial Church in the Inner Quadrangle.

At different times of day in San Francisco, the quality of the light can reduce the city streets (above and below) to monotones, bathe the Bay Bridge (facing page bottom) in mauve, or dramatize the downtown skyline (facing page top and right). Below right: taillights illuminate Lombard Street as it runs towards Telegraph Hill and Coit Tower. Above right: the sun glistens on the ocean beneath the Golden Gate Bridge. Overleaf: skyscrapers along the Embarcadero, and (following page) the sun gilding Golden Gate.